Forces in Motion

by Martin E. Lee

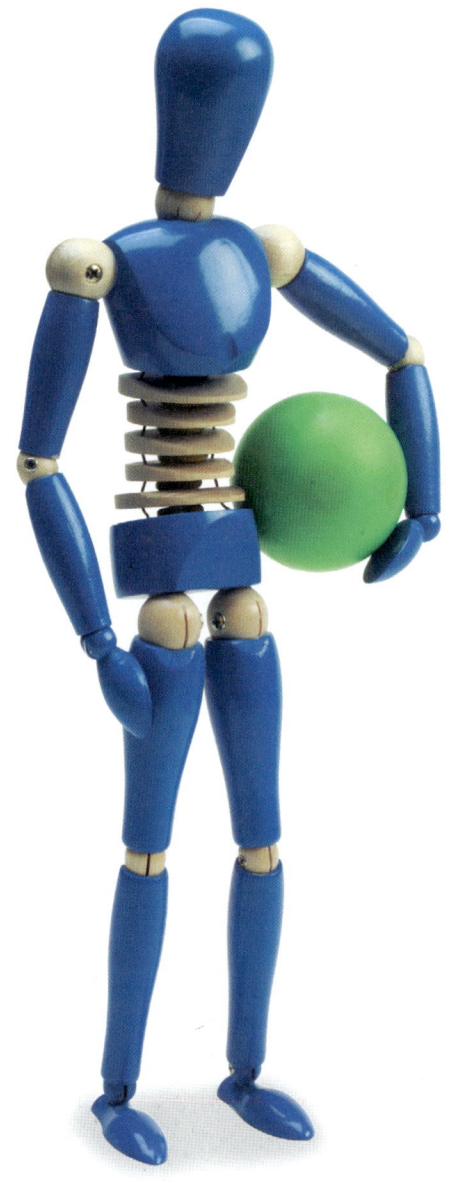

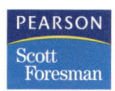 

How can you describe motion?

Types of Motion

You are moving all the time. You walk around your school. You stand up from your chair. You roll over in bed. Your heart beats and your eyelids blink. Motion is also all around you.

Different things move at different rates. A sea star moves very slowly. It may seem as though it is not moving at all. An airplane propeller moves so quickly that you can't even see its blades.

The motion of a sea star is very slow.

There are many different types of motion. Earth is in constant motion. It is always moving as it travels around the Sun. Cars, trucks, and buses have variable motion. They can move in many directions. They can also change their speed. A pendulum has periodic motion. It swings back and forth when it moves. A rubber band has vibrational motion. It vibrates when you pluck it.

This train has variable motion. It can speed up or slow down.

Speed and Velocity

Average speed tells how far an object moves in a certain amount of time. This is the formula for average speed.

$$\text{Speed} = \frac{\text{Distance}}{\text{Time}}$$

Are you in motion when you sit in a chair? You are not moving in relation to the chair. But you are moving in relation to the Sun. You and Earth are moving around the Sun faster than a rocket! To measure motion, you need to look at an object's position when compared to a location. This location is called a point of reference.

Speed changes with the point of reference you use. For example, a woman walking inside of a moving train is moving slowly. The train is moving very quickly. Her motion measured in relation to the end of the train car is one speed. Her speed in relation to a crossing gate next to the tracks is another.

Let's use the end of the train as a point of reference. If the woman walks 10 meters through the train in 5 seconds, she has a walking speed of 2 meters per second.

Now let's use the crossing gate as a new point of reference. Suppose the train is going 30 meters per second. The woman is still walking at the same rate. But with the gate as a point of reference, she is moving about as fast as the train is. So her speed is about 30 meters per second.

Sometimes, knowing the speed of an object is not enough. **Velocity** is the speed of an object in motion and its direction. The speed of the train is 30 meters per second. Its velocity is 30 meters per second north. A skydiver might have a velocity of 200 kilometers per hour downward.

What are forces?

Pushes and Pulls

A **force** is a push or a pull that acts on an object. A force can make an object speed up, slow down, or change its direction.

Forces have magnitude and direction. The magnitude of a force is how strong the force is. It is measured in units called newtons (N). The direction of a force tells which way the force is pushing or pulling. If you hold an apple in your hand, it exerts a downward force with a magnitude of about 1 newton.

Gravity

Every object in the universe pulls on every other one. This pull is called gravity. But only the gravity of a large object such as Earth is strong enough to be felt. Earth's gravity pulls all objects toward it, without even touching them. Pendulums swing, apples fall, and satellites stay in orbit because of the pull of Earth's gravity.

An apple falls because gravity pulls it downward.

Gravity makes the velocity of the apple increase as it falls.

Weight is the amount of gravitational force between an object and Earth. It depends on the mass of the object and the Earth's mass. It also depends on how far above Earth the object is. You weigh a bit less when you fly in an airplane high above Earth. Your weight would be different on other planets. This is because other planets have different masses, so they pull with different amounts of gravitational force. The chart shows how much an object that weighs 100 newtons on Earth would weigh on other planets.

Planet	Weight (in newtons)
Earth	100
Mercury	38
Venus	91
Mars	38
Jupiter	253

Gravity is what makes a pendulum swing downward. The pendulum then swings upward until gravity stops it. Then, as gravity pulls it back down, it swings in the other direction.

Magnetism and Electricity

Magnetism is a force that pushes and pulls objects. The force is strongest at the poles of a magnet. All magnets have a north pole and a south pole. Magnets pull strongly on objects made of iron, cobalt, and nickel. The force of a magnet also works on other magnets. The north pole of one magnet will attract, or pull on, the south pole of another. Two poles that are the same will push each other away.

Electric forces act between objects that have electrical charges. All atoms have electrons, which are negatively charged, and protons, which are positively charged. An object is negatively charged if it gains electrons. It is positively charged if it loses electrons. If you rub silk and glass together, electrons move from the glass to the silk. This gives the glass a positive charge and the silk a negative charge.

All objects with electrical charges push or pull on each other. It is similar to the way magnets work. Objects with opposite charges pull toward each other. Objects with the same charge push away from each other.

The force of the magnet pulls bits of iron toward it.

Gravity, Electricity, and Magnetism

Magnetic and electric forces can act even if the objects do not touch. All these forces get stronger as the objects get closer to each other.

Gravity is different from electricity and magnetism in two important ways. First, you can block the forces of magnetism and electricity. All you have to do is put certain kinds of materials between the objects. But you cannot block gravity. The second difference is in the direction that the forces work. Electricity and magnetism can push or pull on objects. Gravity can only pull on objects.

The magnetic field of this stone attracts metal pins to its surface.

Friction

Friction is the force that results when two materials rub against each other. This force can slow the motion of an object or keep it from moving. Friction depends on the objects that rub together. The shape, speed, or texture of one object can affect the amount of friction with another object. The texture of your socks lets you slide across a smooth floor. But the texture of your shoes does not. There is more friction when you try to slide in your shoes.

Air and water resist motion when moving objects push against them. Air or water flowing over a surface causes friction. Cars and airplanes are designed to cause little friction with the air. Submarines and ships are designed to cause little friction with the water.

The shark's shape and its special skin reduce its friction with water. This helps the shark to swim smoothly and swiftly.

Work and Power

Work has a special meaning in science. **Work** is the energy used when a force moves an object. If an object does not move, no work is done.

Work is calculated by multiplying the force used to move an object by the distance the object is moved.

Work = Force × Distance

Work is measured in units called joules. One joule (J) is the amount of work done when a force of 1 newton (N) moves an object a distance of 1 meter (m).

Power is the rate at which work is done. Power is increased when work is done faster. Walking and running up a hill take the same amount of work. But running up the hill is faster, so it takes more power. Power is measured in units called watts (W). To compute power, divide the amount of work done by the amount of time it takes to do the work.

$$\text{Power} = \frac{\text{Work}}{\text{Time}}$$

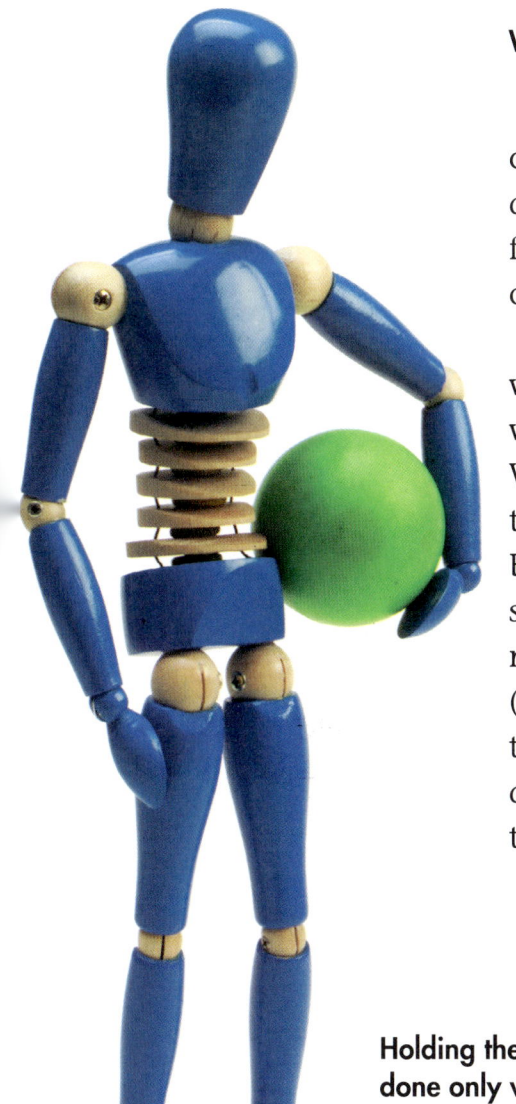

Holding the ball takes force. But work is done only when a force moves an object. Since the ball does not move, no work is being done.

11

What are Newton's laws of motion?

Sir Isaac Newton (1642–1727) was one of the world's most important scientists. His work led to three laws that explain why objects move as they do.

Net Forces

Many forces can act on an object at once. They may act in different directions. Some may be stronger than others. The combined forces on an object is the net force. The net force controls whether the object will start moving, stop moving, or change its direction.

Forces can be balanced. This occurs when equal forces act on an object in opposite directions. When this happens, the net force is zero. An object is in a state of **equilibrium** when all forces acting on it balance each other. A moving object in equilibrium keeps moving at a constant speed in a straight line. A motionless object in equilibrium will not start to move.

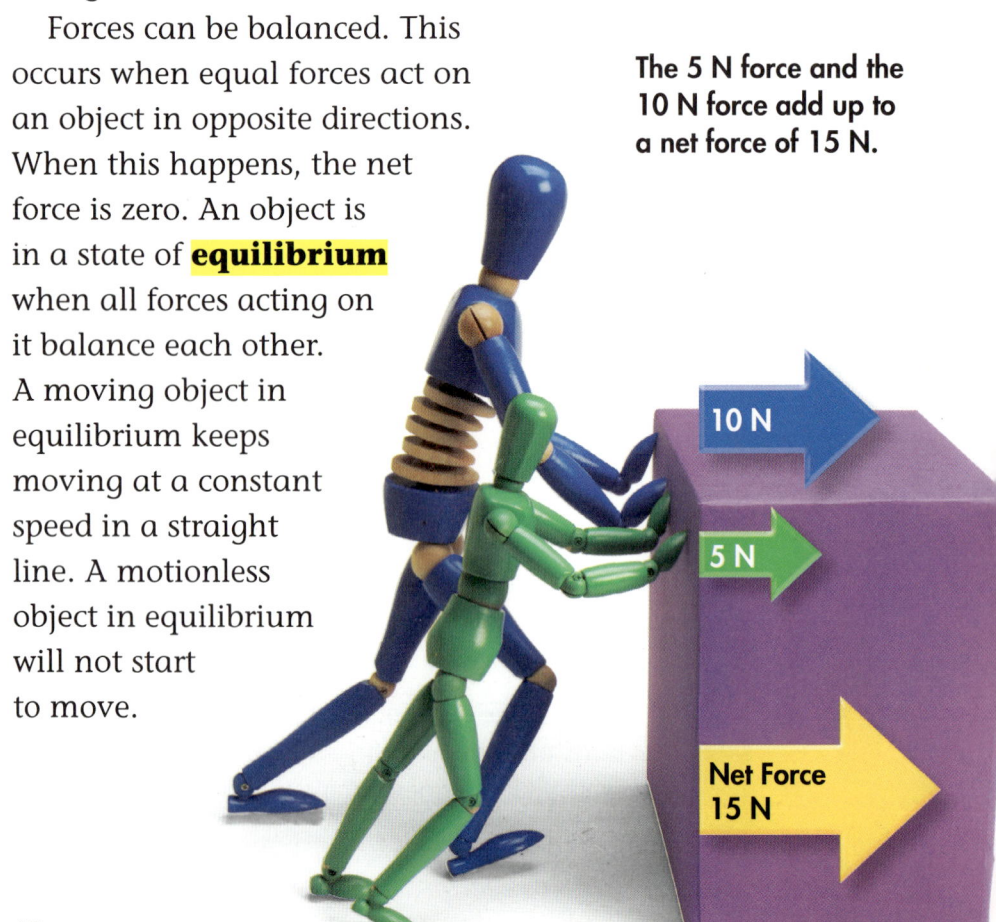

The 5 N force and the 10 N force add up to a net force of 15 N.

Unbalanced forces make an object change its motion. Forces are out of balance if the forces acting in one direction are greater than the forces acting in another. If two people push on a box from opposite directions with the same amount of force, the box will not move. But if one person pushes with more force than the other, the forces are unbalanced. There is a net force in the direction of the stronger push. The box moves in that direction.

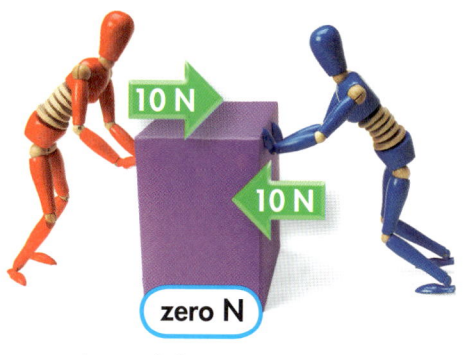

Balanced forces push against the box. There is no net force. The box does not move.

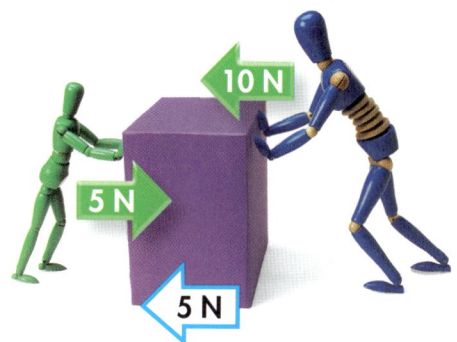

Unbalanced forces push against the box. There is a net force in the direction of the stronger force. The box moves in that direction.

A jet moves in a straight line at a constant speed. But forces are acting on it. Drag pushes against the jet's forward motion. Drag slows it down.

Thrust pushes the jet forward.

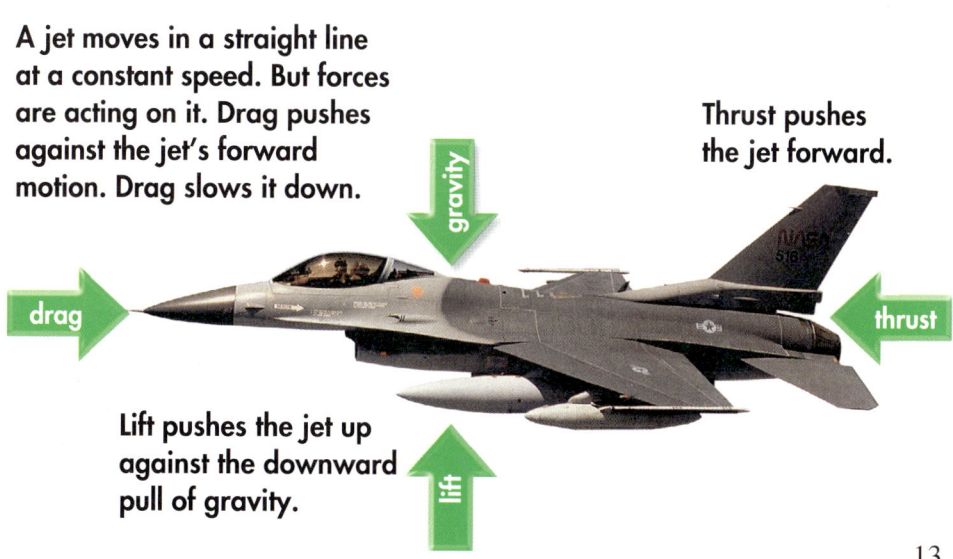

Lift pushes the jet up against the downward pull of gravity.

Newton's First Law

Newton's first law of motion says that an object will stay in constant motion until a net force acts upon it. An object at rest will stay at rest until a net force moves it. An object moving at a constant speed will keep moving in a straight line at that speed. If a net force acts upon it, it can change speed or direction.

Objects tend to resist any change in motion. This is known as **inertia.** Objects with greater mass have more inertia than objects with less mass. Your body's inertia is what pushes you against the side of a car as it goes around a curve. Your body tends to keep moving in a straight line. Then the car turns. It takes a moment for the motion of your body to adjust.

A full truck has more inertia than an empty truck. It will take more effort to make the heavy truck stop or speed up.

Inertia will keep the football moving after the kick. Eventually, gravity will pull the ball to the ground.

The football stays at rest on the tee until the force of the kick causes it to move.

A space probe is an example of Newton's first law. Inertia keeps the probe moving through space. Probes need very little fuel after they get into space. There is no net force to slow them down. They usually need fuel only to change direction or to slow down.

The vehicle stops when it crashes, but the test dummy keeps moving because of inertia. Only the seat belt holds it back.

The net force on the box equals the mass of the box times its acceleration.

The greater the net force on the box, the greater its acceleration will be.

The greater the mass of the box, the less its acceleration will be.

Newton's Second Law

Newton's second law of motion describes how net force, mass, and acceleration are related. **Acceleration** is the rate at which the velocity of an object changes over time. The net forces acting on an object can change its velocity. You may think of accelerating as speeding up. But acceleration can mean speeding up, slowing down, or changing direction.

This formula shows Newton's second law of motion.

Force = Mass × Acceleration

The formula can be written as

$F = m \times a.$

To find an object's acceleration, the formula can be written as

$a = \dfrac{F}{m}.$

To find the mass of an object, the formula is written as

$m = \dfrac{F}{a}.$

Newton's Third Law

Newton's third law of motion states that when one object pushes or pulls on another, the second object pushes or pulls back on the first object. This is also called the action-reaction law of motion. Action-reaction forces are always equal and opposite. They always come in pairs.

You can see this law at work every day. When you see an object move because of a force, there will also be an equal and opposite force. It is impossible to have one force without an equal and opposite force!

Have you ever ridden in a bumper car? A moving car may bump into a stopped car. Both drivers will feel the force of the impact. The force slows down the moving car and puts the stopped car in motion.

Bumper cars exert equal and opposite forces on each other.

What are simple machines?

Machines and Work

A **machine** is a device that changes the direction or amount of force needed to do work. Simple machines have only a few parts. Four simple machines are the pulley, the wheel and axle, the lever, and the inclined plane.

Machines do not reduce the amount of work that needs to be done. They can make it easier to do the work. A machine can allow you to use less force to do work. In exchange, you must apply that force over a greater distance. This balance lets the total amount of work stay the same. A machine might make work easier by changing the direction of the force.

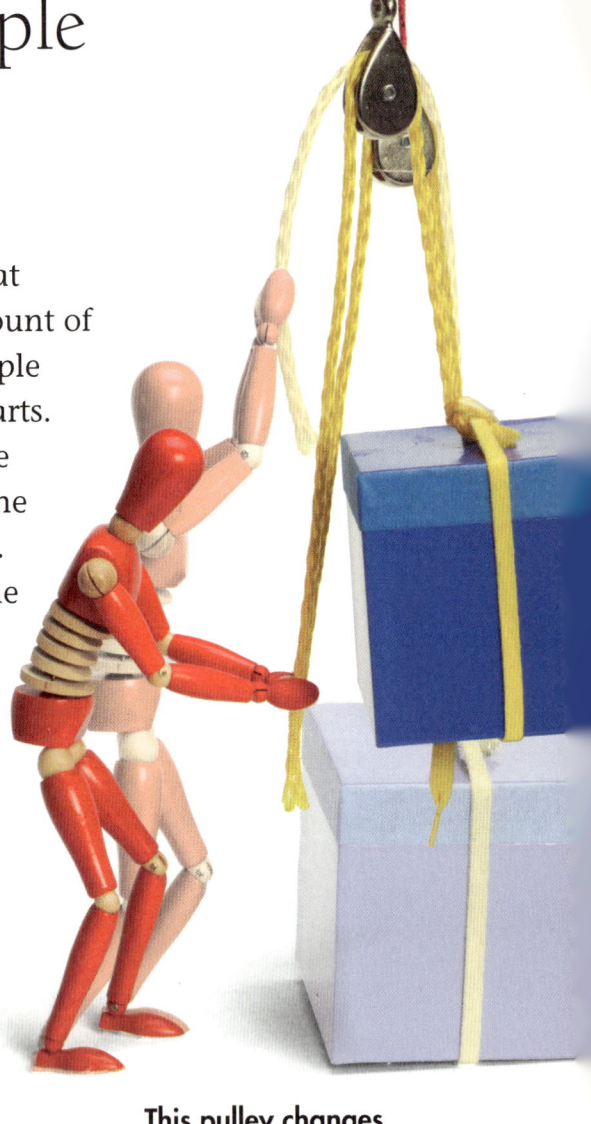

This pulley changes the direction of force.

Pulley

A pulley is one type of simple machine that changes the direction of the force needed. A pulley is a rope or cable that runs around a grooved wheel. Flagpoles use pulleys. So do some kinds of curtains. A block and tackle is a system of pulleys. The block and tackle can make it easier to lift heavy objects.

Wheel and Axle

A wheel and axle has a round object, such as a doorknob, and a shaft. The wheel and axle reduces the amount of force needed to do work. Think how hard it would be to pull a bucket of water up and out of a well. Instead of pulling the bucket in a straight line, you turn the crank in a circle. The steering wheel of a car is another kind of wheel and axle.

The crank on this well is a kind of wheel and axle.

Lever

A lever is another simple machine that changes the direction of a force. A lever has a bar that rotates on a fixed point. That fixed point is called the fulcrum. Levers use the bar, the fulcrum, and a force that you apply to move a load.

A see-saw is a lever that changes the direction of force. To use a see-saw to lift a box, you push down at one end. The box goes up at the other end. The amount of force needed to move the box will change if you change the position of the fulcrum. The farther you are from the fulcrum, the easier it is to push down on the lever.

Look at the picture below of the person using a lever to lift a box. The person applies less force than the weight of the box. But the person must apply that force for 1 m. The box rises only 0.5 m.

Other Simple Levers

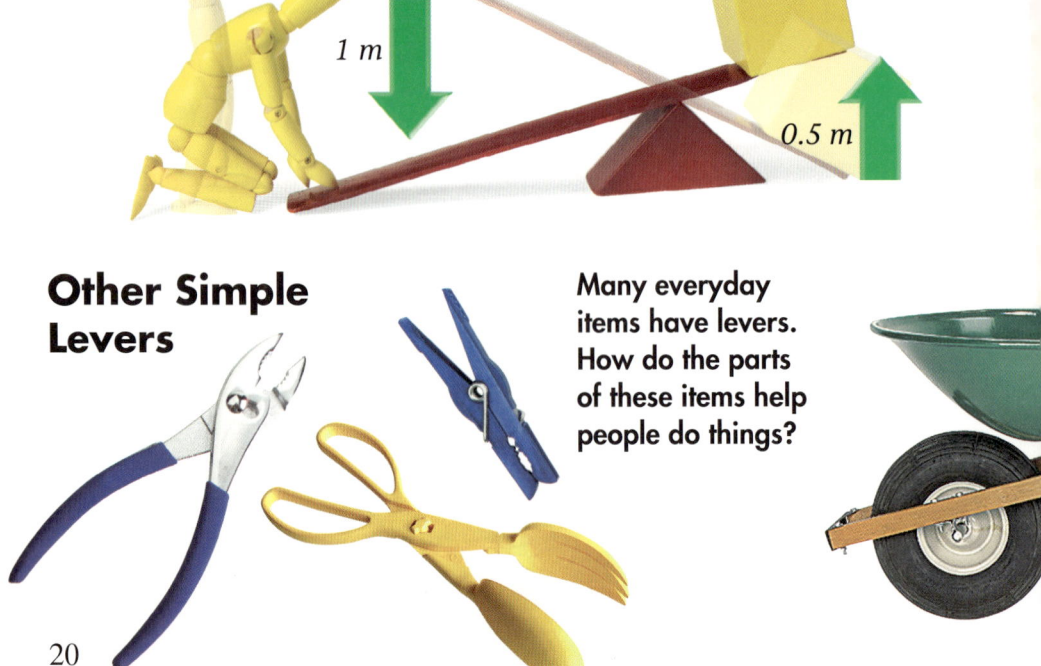

Many everyday items have levers. How do the parts of these items help people do things?

Inclined Planes

Have you ever carried something heavy up a flight of stairs? Rolling the load up a ramp would be much easier. A ramp is a type of simple machine called an inclined plane. It is a flat surface with one end higher than the other. The inclined plane can be a big ramp that a car might go up. Or it can be a small wedge such as a doorstop.

Pushing a wheelchair up a ramp uses less force over a longer distance than lifting it up the steps.

21

Complex Machines

Many machines combine two or more simple machines. These are called complex machines. They might use burning fuel, gravity, human power, electricity, or magnetism to do work. Look at the picture of the go-cart. It uses many simple machines to move the driver along.

A go-cart is a complex machine.

The go cart's steering wheel is a wheel and axle. This simple machine is connected to levers that turn the front wheels. The pedals the driver uses to control the engine and brakes are also levers. Gears, a type of wheel and axle system, connect the engine to the cart's rear wheels. The engine itself is a complex machine. It is made up of many small simple machines.

Glossary

acceleration — the rate at which the velocity of an object changes over time

equilibrium — a state in which all forces acting on an object balance each other

force — a push or a pull that acts on an object

inertia — the tendency of an object to resist any change in motion

machine — a device that changes the direction of force or the amount of force needed to do work

power — the rate at which work is done

velocity — the speed and direction of an object's motion

work — the energy used when a force moves an object